C000016367

Projects
for
programs

written by DEREK BLEASE, M Phil, B A, Cert Ed
Department of Education,
Loughborough University of Technology

Ladybird Books Loughborough

READ THIS BEFORE YOU BEGIN. IT'S IMPORTANT!

Using arrays

Make sure that you understand what an array is and how it works. You will also need to understand how to use FOR-TO-NEXT loops to both READ DATA into an array and to PRINT out the contents. It would be useful to consult the other books in this series to help you to understand how to improve your programs by improving screen layout, adding graphics, colour and sound.

Each project will help you to understand a little more about the ways in which arrays work and can be used in a variety of programs.

Program design

The suggested program designs in each of the projects fall roughly into five parts:

1 DIMension the arrays
2 Enter or READ in the DATA
3 The main control program
4 The major SUBROUTINES
5 The DATA (except where data is entered from the keyboard)

Once the array has been DIMensioned and the DATA entered, the main control program organises the use of the subroutines. These all appear after the control program so that they are easy to find.

This style of structured programming has been adopted so that the programs are easier to follow and relate to the flow diagrams. They can be easily modified to suit a variety of computers, eg subroutines converted to PROCEDURES for BBC computer users.

It is *important* to remember that the best programs are thought out fully and written down on paper before they are typed into the computer.

Crashproof your programs

When you come to try the program suggestions in this book you will soon find that if you type in the wrong thing the program will CRASH! Before you finally use your programs you will need to add extra lines of your own to trap these errors. The best way to test for errors is to go through each program deliberately typing in the wrong responses until you are satisfied that nothing you do will make the program go wrong. This is particularly important if you ever plan to use for example the computer scoreboard program (see page 24) in a real competition.

Stories, jokes and poems

Have you ever thought what fun it would be if you could get your computer to do your English homework? Many computer games depend on the computer's ability to fit pieces of information together at random. They create the illusion that they can think up an infinite number of different mazes, monsters or secret passages to trap the unwary games player. What is really happening is that the computer is putting together a small number of pieces of DATA in a fixed pattern. The illusion is created by giving the computer a number of different possibilities to choose from at each stage. The more possibilities, the greater the variety of outcomes.

So that you can understand how this works we will start with a simple program to write variations on a famous nonsense poem by Lewis Carroll. The poem is called *The Jabberwocky* and the first verse goes like this:

> *'Twas brillig, and the slithy toves*
> *Did gyre and gimble in the wabe:*
> *All mimsy were the borogoves,*
> *And the mome raths outgrabe.*

In line 1 there are two phrases, *Twas brillig* and *slithy toves*, which we could change and think up all sorts of amusing phrases to take their place. We could call these RANDOM PHRASES. These are joined together by *and the*, which is a CONNECTING PHRASE which will never change.

In line 2 the random phrases are *did gyre and gimble* and *wabe*. The connecting phrase is *in the*.

We could put all of the connecting phrases together in one array A$(4) and all the random phrases together in another array B$(9,N). This would mean that in each verse there were four connecting phrases and N possible choices for each of nine random phrases. If we start with just two choices, the two arrays would look like this:

Connecting phrases A$(4)	Random phrases B$(9,2)	Alternative random phrases
(1) and the	(1) 'twas brillig	'tis wally
(2) in the	(2) slithy toves	writhy stoves
(3) were the	(3) did gyre and gimble	did slide and slither
(4) and the	(4) wabe	crabe
	(5) All mimsy	So flippy
	(6) borogoves	earthy loaves
	(7) mome	tome
	(8) raths	nurgs
	(9) outgrabe	imlabe

Slithy tove!!

Note that if you are using Sinclair BASIC the two arrays must include an element to indicate the maximum length of each string, including all spaces.

For example A$(4,10) would allow connecting phrases up to 10 characters in length. B$(9,2,25) would allow random phrases up to 25 characters in length.

Here is the program listing.

4

```
10 REM ********************************
20 REM**VARIATIONS ON THE JABBERWOCKY**
30 REM**BY LEWIS CARROLL 1832-1899**
40REM ********************************
50 REM --------------------------------
60 REM DIMension arrays and READ DATA
70 REM --------------------------------
80 DIM A$(4):DIM B$(9,2)
90 FOR R=1 TO 4: READ A$(R):NEXT R
100 FOR R=1 TO 9: FOR C=1 TO 2
110 READ B$(R,C):NEXT C:NEXT R
120 REM --------------------------------
130 REM Set values of A and B to zero
140 REM and clear screen
150 REM --------------------------------
160 A=0:B=0:CLS
170 REM --------------------------------
180 REM PRINT lines 1,2 and 3
190 REM --------------------------------
200 FOR P=1 TO 3
210 GOSUB 420
220 GOSUB 460
230 GOSUB 510
240 GOSUB 610
250 A=A+1
260 GOSUB 460
270 GOSUB 560
280 NEXT P
290 REM --------------------------------
300 REM PRINT line 4
310 REM --------------------------------
320 GOSUB 420
330 GOSUB 610
340 FOR A=7 TO 9:GOSUB 460
350 GOSUB 510
360 NEXT A
370 PRINT
380 END
390 REM --------------------------------
400 REM Reset values of A and B
410 REM --------------------------------
420 A=A+1:B=B+1:RETURN
430 REM --------------------------------
440 REM Random number routine
450 REM --------------------------------
460 X=RND(2):RETURN
470 REM --------------------------------
480 REM PRINT random phrase
490 REM without starting new line
500 REM --------------------------------
510 PRINT B$(A,X);:RETURN
520 REM --------------------------------
530 REM PRINT random phrase
540 REM and start new line
550 REM --------------------------------
560 PRINT B$(A,X):RETURN
570 REM --------------------------------
580 REM PRINT connecting phrase
590 REM without starting new line
600 REM --------------------------------
610 PRINT A$(B);:RETURN
620 DATA "and the ","in the ","were the "
630 DATA " and the ","'Twas brillig, "
640 DATA "'Tis wally, ","slithy toves "
650 DATA "writhy stoves "," Did gyre and gimble "
660 DATA " Did slide and slither ","wabe:","crabe:"
670 DATA "All mimsy ","So flippy ","borogoves,"
680 DATA "earthy loaves,","mome ","tome ","raths "
690 DATA "nurgs ","outgrabe.","imlabe."
```

Notice that the arrays are DIMensioned at line 80 and a FOR-TO-NEXT loop is used to READ the DATA which appears at the end of the program.

Sinclair users, don't forget to change line 80 to this:

80 DIM A$(4,10): DIM B$(9,2,25)

If you type in this program you will see that each RUN gives a slightly different variation on the original poem. However, they are all fairly similar because we only allowed two choices of random phrase at each stage.

It is the SUBROUTINE at line 460 which makes the choices by selecting random numbers. These random numbers correspond to the column numbers in the array B$(9,2). If we were to increase the size of B$(9,2) to B$(9,5), then line 460 would have to change to X = RND(5). We would also have to think up another three variations for each of the nine random phrases. You can have as many alternatives as you can invent, but when you make them up be sure you know which ones must rhyme.

Setting out the poem

When you plan a program of this kind it is important to know which phrases appear in the middle, and which phrases appear at the end of a line. Look at lines 510 and 560. You will notice that the only difference is a semi-colon (;). If the program calls on line 510, the next phrase will be printed on the same line. If it calls on line 560 to do the same job, the next phrase will be printed on the next line.

You will need to arrange your PRINT commands in such a way that you start new lines in the right places. Here is a flow-diagram to show you how this program is organised:

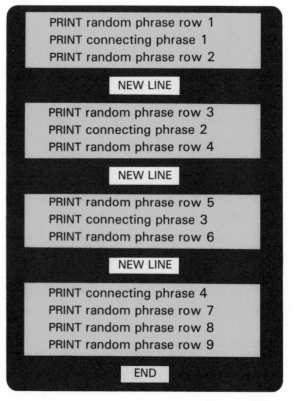

PRINT random phrase row 1
PRINT connecting phrase 1
PRINT random phrase row 2

NEW LINE

PRINT random phrase row 3
PRINT connecting phrase 2
PRINT random phrase row 4

NEW LINE

PRINT random phrase row 5
PRINT connecting phrase 3
PRINT random phrase row 6

NEW LINE

PRINT connecting phrase 4
PRINT random phrase row 7
PRINT random phrase row 8
PRINT random phrase row 9

END

Of course for the other verses and other poems or stories the flow diagram would be different. If you start off by setting it out in this way you will find it easier to see how to organise your own program.

Spaces, punctuation and indents

Look at lines 620 to 690. They contain the DATA. All of the spaces and punctuation are included within the inverted commas. If you do not type them in correctly your poem will not be properly set out. Even the indents at the beginnings of the second and fourth lines of the poem are included as spaces in the DATA.

Some ideas to try

1 Increase the number of alternatives in array A$(9,2) so that your poems have more variety. You will need to look closely at lines 80, 90, 100 and 460.

2 Find a copy of the complete poem and extend the program to write variations on each verse in turn. Then print them out as a complete poem.

3 Design a program to write random limericks. Start off with a limerick that you know. Decide which will be your RANDOM PHRASES and which will be your CONNECTING PHRASES. Then you can think up some alternative random phrases.

Here is a limerick written by Edward Lear, to help you to get started:

There was an old man with a beard,
Who said, 'It is just as I feared!
Two owls and a hen,
Four larks and a wren,
Have all built their nests in my beard!'

4 Design a program that will write stories!

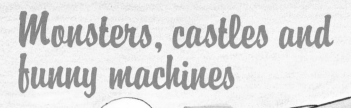

Monsters, castles and funny machines

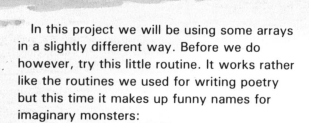

In this project we will be using some arrays in a slightly different way. Before we do however, try this little routine. It works rather like the routines we used for writing poetry but this time it makes up funny names for imaginary monsters:

```
10 DIM D$(4,6)
20 FOR R=1 TO 4: FOR C=1 TO 6
30 READ D$(R,C): NEXT C:NEXT R
40 PRINT "The:"
50 FOR C=1 TO 6: R=RND(4)
60 PRINT D$(R,C);
70 NEXT C
80 PRINT
90 DATA Hyfer,lootin,hootin
100 DATA tootin,gargl,flopper
110 DATA Super,rattlin,inter
120 DATA puffin,hobble,closter
130 DATA Ankle,dustin,rapid
140 DATA rustin,tarmac,eater
150 DATA Over,steamin,thunder
160 DATA lightnin,sparkl,buster
```

8

Notice that the DATA is stored at the end, so that it is easy to make changes or additions. You could enlarge this program by increasing the size of D$(4,6) and making up some more DATA. If you are not using BBC BASIC you will need to use inverted commas in the data lines but spaces are not necessary.

Sinclair users must remember to define the maximum string length in line 10.

See if you can write a similar routine for the name of a haunted castle, or for the name of a funny machine which seems to describe what it does. You might find these routines useful later on, so keep them handy.

Making the computer ask questions

Another way to load data into an array is to use INPUT commands. This way the computer can be made to ask questions. If we are careful about what questions it asks and what comments it makes, we can create the illusion that the computer can think for itself. You could even store your questions in an array and use the random number routine to select them. This way even you wouldn't know which question was going to come up next. The answers to the questions can be stored in another array. If some of those answers are going to be numbers, they could go in a separate numerical array and be used in calculations if you wished. The functions VAL and STR$ may be useful here also, so if you are not sure what they do, then consult your *User Manual* to find out.

Let us start with a simple example. The computer is going to ask these four questions about a monster:

1 What colour is the monster?
2 Where are its eyes?
3 How many ears has it got?
4 How tall is it?

Can you think up similar questions for your haunted castle and your funny machine?

Questions 1 and 2 require answers in words which must be stored in a string array. Questions 3 and 4 require answers in numbers which could be stored in a numerical array, or converted to strings using STR$.

Wording the questions

You need to make sure that the answers to the questions can be easily fitted together into sentences. This will make the final printout routine easier. It is probably best to phrase the questions carefully giving instructions to help. One way to do this is to start the answer off like this:

Question 1 *What is the colour of the monster?*
The monster is....

If you would prefer all answers to be in words you could always use this little routine to convert the words to numbers:

```
10 GOSUB 40
20 PRINT E$,E
30 END
40 REM ----------------------------
50 REM WORDS TO NUMBERS ROUTINE
60 REM ----------------------------
70 INPUT "How many ears has it got",E$
80 IF E$="NONE" THEN E=0:RETURN
90 IF E$="ONE" THEN E=1:RETURN
100 IF E$="TWO" THEN E=2:RETURN
110 IF E$="THREE" THEN E=3:RETURN
120 PRINT "Try something between ";
130 PRINT "none and three."
140 GOTO 70
```

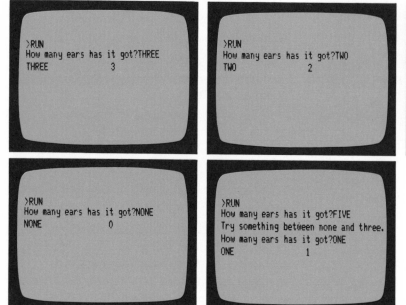

```
>RUN
How many ears has it got?THREE
THREE          3
```

```
>RUN
How many ears has it got?TWO
TWO            2
```

```
>RUN
How many ears has it got?ONE
ONE            1
```

```
>RUN
How many ears has it got?NONE
NONE           0
```

```
>RUN
How many ears has it got?FIVE
Try something between none and three.
How many ears has it got?ONE
ONE            1
```

Line 20 simply prints out the word and number to help you to see how the program works. Normally you would store the number in an array for later use.

10

Funny Comments

You can continue the illusion that the computer can think by making it comment on the answers you type in to its questions. Let's look again at our question 1 about the colour of the monster. The program could be:

```
10 PRINT "What colour is the monster?"
20 INPUT "The monster is....";C$
```

Now you can program the computer to make different comments depending upon the colour chosen. Try this:

```
10 PRINT "What colour is the monster?"
20 INPUT "The monster is...",C$
30 IF C$="RED" THEN PRINT "I think
   your monster blushes easily.":GOTO 80
40 IF C$="BLUE" THEN PRINT "Perhaps
   he doesn't like the cold.":GOTO 80
50 IF C$="GREEN" THEN PRINT "Perhaps
   he's feeling seasick.":GOTO 80
60 IF C$="YELLOW" THEN PRINT "It's all
   that custard he eats.":GOTO 80
70 PRINT "That's an unusual colour,
   did he choose it himself?"
80 END
```

Try this idea. Develop this program so that for each colour there are several alternative comments stored in an array. The comments can be chosen using a random number routine so that you can never be sure which one will come up next. Now try this design with some different questions and comments about your haunted castle or funny machine.

11

Searching for words

If you want to see if a single word appears in a longer string then the function INSTR is very useful. Here is how it is used:

```
10 PRINT "What colour is the monster?"
20 INPUT "The monster is ...",A$
30 B$="GREEN"
40 X=INSTR(A$,B$)
50 IF X>0 THEN PRINT "Well I see there
   are some green bits anyway.";
```

```
>RUN
What colour is the monster?
The monster is ...?PINK WITH GREENISH
SPOTS
Well I see there are some green
bits anyway.
```

In this example the colour GREEN is picked out from the PINK WITH GREENISH SPOTS. If the word had not been there the value of X would have been zero. If the reply does include GREEN the value of X becomes the position of its first letter (G). In this case it would be the number 11 because G is the eleventh character, including spaces. If X is any number greater than zero the word GREEN must be in there somewhere.

Add these extra lines to the last example and see what happens:

```
60 B$="SPOTS"
70 X=INSTR(A$,B$)
80 IF X>0 THEN PRINT "I'm sure the
   spots are really quite pretty."
90 B$="STRIPES"
100 X=INSTR(A$,B$)
110 IF X>0 THEN PRINT "I'm not so sure
    about the stripes.":GOTO 130
120 PRINT "I'm glad there are no
    stripes!"
130 END
```

Sinclair BASIC does not include an INSTR function, and so a little routine written in BASIC must be used instead. Try this one. It searches for the substring B$ in the larger string A$. If it finds it the word YES appears on the screen:

```
10 INPUT A$
20 INPUT B$
30 LET A=LEN A$
40 LET B=LEN B$
50 FOR X=1 TO (A−2)
60 IF A$(X TO (X+B−1))=B$ THEN PRINT
   "YES"
70 NEXT X
```

Storing the replies in an array

First of all decide what questions you want the computer to ask. Then you can include an array large enough to store the answers as they are typed in. This time we DIMension the array but do not include any line of DATA in the program. As each answer is typed in, it is stored as a string in the next available space in the array. If the array has two dimensions, (Rows and Columns), you could also store the funny comments. You could try that for yourself. The array for our monster program might look like this:

The array would be Q$(4) (Q = Questions).

Q$

What colour is the monster?	(1)	RED
Where are its eyes?	(2)	ON ITS NOSE
How many ears has it got?	(3)	FOUR
How tall is it?	(4)	AS TALL AS A BUS

So Q$(1) is "RED"
Q$(2) is "ON ITS NOSE"
Q$(3) is "FOUR"
Q$(4) is "AS TALL AS A BUS"

13

Printing out the data

If you just want to check the contents of the array then use this simple routine. Make sure you understand how it works; you'll need to use it a lot in some later projects:

```
10 FOR N = 1 TO 4
20 PRINT Q$(N)
30 NEXT N
```

Of course that does not print it out in a way that makes much sense so you will have to print out each row of your array separately, adding suitable connecting phrases as you go. Here is a very simple example:

```
500 PRINT ''The terrible monster is ''
        ;Q$(1);''all over''
510 PRINT ''with its beady eyes stuck on its ''
        ;Q$(2);''.''
520 PRINT ''It listens to our every sound
        with its '';Q$(3);'' ears''
530 PRINT ''and it is '';Q$(4);''.''
```

If you add your monster name routine, you could start the whole printout with a different humorous name every time.

Some ideas to try

1 Write three programs: one about a monster, one about a castle and one about a funny machine. For each program store the replies and funny comments in an array. Print out a full description of each at the end.

2 When you have got all three programs working, combine their routines into a single program about a monster who lives in a castle and owns a funny machine.

14

A data-base for collectors

Have you ever thought how useful it would be to keep information stored on a computer file instead of in a book? Some people keep whole telephone directories on computer files. If they want to find a number, all they have to do is to type in the person's name or their address. It is even possible to type in a telephone number and the computer will print out the name and address of its owner. If you were in a hurry, this kind of data file would save a lot of time.

Of course you could keep other kinds of information in data files: details of your stamp collection, bus, car or train numbers, details of your record collection, or the top 20 records in the hit parade. There are many possibilities but they all have one thing in common. Each FILE is made up of a collection of ITEMS. For example, in a FILE of cars each car is a separate ITEM. So if there are 20 cars there are 20 ITEMS. Each item has a number of FIELDS, that is separate pieces of information about it. If each ITEM is a car, then its FIELDS might be: *1 MAKE, 2 COLOUR, 3 REGISTRATION NUMBER* and *4 YEAR OF MANUFACTURE*, making four FIELDS in all.

Information of this kind is best stored in a two-dimensional array having several ROWS (for the ITEMS), and several COLUMNS (for the FIELDS).

Here is an example of a file of cars with four ITEMS and the four FIELDS.

FILE: CARS

		FIELDS			
		MAKE	*COLOUR*	*REG. No.*	*YEAR*
	1	ROVER	RED	MAY781F	1967
ITEMS	2	FORD	BLUE	AVA212Y	1982
	3	MORRIS	GREEN	CRY683T	1979
	4	FIAT	WHITE	LUT232V	1980

```
10 CLS
20 REM *****A SIMPLE DATABASE******
30 REM *CONTAINING ONLY ONE FIELD**
40 REM ****************************
50 REM --------------------------
60 REM INPUT ROUTINE
70 REM --------------------------
80 INPUT "HOW MANY ITEMS ",N
90 DIM A$(N)
100 FOR M=1 TO N
110 PRINT "WHAT IS ITEM NUMBER ";M
120 INPUT A$(M)
130 NEXT M
140 REM --------------------------
150 REM PRINTOUT ROUTINE
160 REM --------------------------
170 FOR M=1 TO N
180 PRINT "ITEM ";M;" ";A$(M)
190 NEXT M
200 INPUT "ANY CHANGES (Y OR N)",R$
210 IF R$="Y" THEN 260
220 IF R$="N" THEN 330 ELSE 200
230 REM --------------------------
240 REM CHANGES ROUTINE
250 REM --------------------------
260 PRINT"WHICH ITEM DO YOU WANT TO CHANGE?"
270 INPUT M
280 PRINT "TYPE IN THE NEW ITEM ";M
290 INPUT A$(M)
300 INPUT "ANY MORE CHANGES (Y OR N)",R$
310 IF R$="Y"THEN 260
320 IF R$="N" THEN 170 ELSE 300
330 END
```

If we called this array C$ then it would be DEFined as C$(4,4).

C$(2,1) would be 'FORD', and C$(2,4) would be its year of manufacture, '1982'.

Here is a program for a simple data-base which has only one field. All it does is to print a simple list:

16

Notice that it has three main parts. An INPUT routine, a PRINTOUT routine and a CHANGES routine. Make sure that you understand how these work. Type the program into your computer and try it.

Remember, if you are using Sinclair BASIC you will have to change line 90 to define the maximum string length, also line 220 and 230 will have to be changed to:

220 IF R$ = "N" THEN GOTO 330
225 GOTO 200

and

320 IF R$ = "N" THEN GOTO 170
325 GOTO 300

As you experiment with this program you will find that you can type in quite long strings. What do you think would be the maximum length? Consult your computer handbook if you do not know.

Here is a typical sample-run. It will help you to understand how the three sections work. Notice how useful it is to have a changes routine. Remember, the computer will not allow you to re-DIMension the array A$(N) once you have started. You cannot add extra items but you can replace existing ones.

```
HOW MANY ITEMS ?4
WHAT IS ITEM NUMBER 1
?ROVER
```

```
WHAT IS ITEM NUMBER 2
?FORD
```

```
WHAT IS ITEM NUMBER 3
?MORRIS
```

```
WHAT IS ITEM NUMBER 4
?FIAT
```

```
ITEM 1 ROVER
ITEM 2 FORD
ITEM 3 MORRIS
ITEM 4 FIAT
ANY CHANGES (Y OR N)?Y
```

```
WHICH ITEM DO YOU WANT TO CHANGE?
?1
TYPE IN THE NEW ITEM 1
?ROVER 2000 TC
```

```
ANY MORE CHANGES (Y OR N)?Y
WHICH ITEM DO YOU WANT TO CHANGE?
?2
TYPE IN THE NEW ITEM 2
?FORD CORTINA GHIA
```

```
ANY MORE CHANGES (Y OR N)?Y
WHICH ITEM DO YOU WANT TO CHANGE?
?3
TYPE IN THE NEW ITEM 3
?MORRIS MINIVAN
```

```
ANY MORE CHANGES (Y OR N)?Y
WHICH ITEM DO YOU WANT TO CHANGE?
?4
TYPE IN THE NEW ITEM 4
?FIAT 500
```

```
ANY MORE CHANGES (Y OR N)?N
ITEM 1 ROVER 2000 TC
ITEM 2 FORD CORTINA GHIA
ITEM 3 MORRIS MINIVAN
ITEM 4 FIAT 500
ANY CHANGES (Y OR N)?N
```

Of course this program is not very useful because it only has one FIELD of information for each ITEM, nor does it allow us to ask it questions about the data. Here is a flow diagram to show you one way to organise a more useful data-base program:

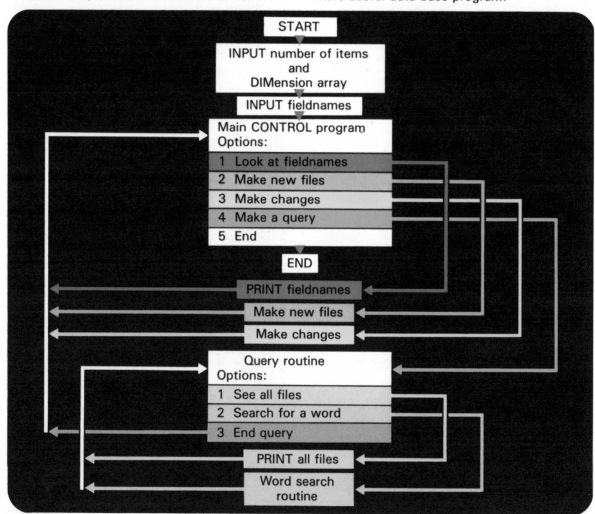

Notice that once the array is DIMensioned and the fieldnames are entered, the whole thing is organised by the main control program. This offers five options. Each time a choice is made, the computer jumps to the chosen sub-routine and then returns to the control program.

Notice that the array has two DIMensions, A$(N items, 2 fields), and that in line 120 the fieldnames are stored in row 0. The reason for this is simple. If we store the fieldnames in row 0 then the row numbers will be the same as the ITEM numbers. Row 1 = item 1, row 2 = item 2 and so on.

A data-base with two fields

Here is an input routine for two fields.

If you are using Sinclair BASIC you will have to change this because all subscripts begin at 1, not zero. You will need to do this throughout your program.

```
10 REM*******A SIMPLE DATABASE*****
20 REM****CONTAINING TWO FIELDS****
30 REM*****************************
40 CLS
50 REM -------------------------
60 REM INPUT ITEMS AND FIELDS
70 REM -------------------------
80 INPUT "HOW MANY ITEMS ",N
90 DIM A$(N,2)
100 FOR M=1 TO 2
110 PRINT "WHAT IS THE NAME OF FIELD No. ";M
120 INPUT A$(0,M)
130 NEXT M
```

The number of FIELDS can be changed by altering lines 90 and 100.

19

The main control program

The main control program allows you to choose from five options:

```
140 REM ------------------------
150 REM**SELECT OPTIONS ROUTINE**
160 REM ------------------------
170 PRINT "DO YOU WANT TO:"
180 PRINT
190 PRINT "1.LOOK AT THE FIELDNAMES?"
200 PRINT "2.MAKE NEW FILES?"
210 PRINT "3.MAKE CHANGES?"
220 PRINT "4.MAKE A QUERY?"
230 PRINT "5. END?"
240 INPUT S
250 ON S GOSUB 280,370,490,700,270
260 GOTO 150
```

Sinclair users will have to change line 250 using IF – THEN – GOSUB.

Try this routine for making new files:

```
360 REM ------------------------
370 REM**MAKE NEW FILES ROUTINE**
380 REM ------------------------
390 FOR R=1 TO N
400 CLS
410 PRINT "WHAT IS ITEM No.";R
420 INPUT A$(R,0)
430 FOR M=1 TO 2
440 PRINT "FIELD:";A$(0,M);":IS";
450 INPUT A$(R,M)
460 NEXT M:NEXT R
470 RETURN
```

Notice that this time column 0 has been used to store the FIELDNAMES.

In Sinclair BASIC this will be column 1.

This is what the array will look like if we have just four items:

	0	1	2
0		Fieldname 1	Fieldname 2
1	item 1		
2	item 2		
3	item 3		
4	item 4		

In Sinclair BASIC the array will look like this:

	1	2	3
1		Fieldname 1	Fieldname 2
2	item 1		
3	item 2		
4	item 3		
5	item 4		

Alternatively the ITEMS and FIELDNAMES could be stored in a separate array.

By now you should be able to add your own routines to look at the fieldnames (from line 270), and to make changes (from line 480).

Asking questions – the query routine

This part of the program is known as the QUERY routine. Like the main control program it offers a choice.

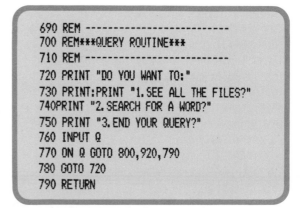

```
690 REM ------------------------
700 REM***QUERY ROUTINE***
710 REM ------------------------
720 PRINT "DO YOU WANT TO:"
730 PRINT:PRINT "1.SEE ALL THE FILES?"
740PRINT "2.SEARCH FOR A WORD?"
750 PRINT "3.END YOUR QUERY?"
760 INPUT Q
770 ON Q GOTO 800,920,790
780 GOTO 720
790 RETURN
```

Write your own SEE ALL FILES routine (from line 800) and then try this WORD SEARCH routine:

```
910 REM -------------------------
920 REM **WORD SEARCH**
930 REM -------------------------
940 CLS
950 PRINT "THE AVAILABLE FIELDS ARE:"
960 FOR M=1 TO 2
970 PRINT A$(0,M)
980 NEXT M
990 PRINT "WHICH WORD WOULD YOU LIKE TO SEARCH?"
1000 INPUT W$
1010 FOR R=1 TO N
1020 FOR M=1 TO 2
1030 IF W$=A$(R,M) THEN 1070
1040 NEXT M
1050 NEXT R
1060 RETURN
1070 PRINT A$(R,0)
1080 PRINT A$(0,1);":";A$(R,1)
1090 PRINT A$(0,2);":";A$(R,2)
1100 GOTO 1040
```

It starts by telling us the FIELDNAMES and then asks for a word or words to be typed in, (W$). It then goes through each box of the array, row by row, to see whether W$ occurs in any of them. If it does, lines 1070 to 1090 print out the complete row. It then continues until the search is completed.

Saving files on tape or disc

Once you have got your data-base program to work you will want to keep your files for future use. Data-files are usually stored on tape or disc. You will need to write two short routines. The first one will be to save the contents of the array on tape or disc. Different computers may use different commands for this so you will need to consult your *User Manual*. The second routine will be to load data from your files into the array. To help you to find the right commands for your computer, here are some examples:

BBC, Tandy etc   PRINT # AND INPUT #

SINCLAIR   SAVE DATA and LOAD DATA

Remember, when you load a file, the first item of data must always be the number of items in the file. This will enable the computer to DIMension the array to the right size to hold all of the data.

Where to put your SAVE and LOAD routines

You will need to choose between the LOAD FILES and the INPUT ITEMS and FIELDS routines at the beginning of the program.

You could use lines 10 to 40 for this:

```
10 PRINT "New data or old?"
20 INPUT D$
30 IF D$ = "OLD" THEN GOTO 1110
40 IF D$<>"NEW" THEN GOTO 10
```

Your LOAD FILES routine can then begin at line 1110 and end with GOTO 150.

The SAVE FILES routine should be offered as an extra option in the SELECT OPTIONS routine and the subroutine can go at the end of the program.

WHAT A LOT OF IDEAS THIS CAN BE USED FOR!

Some ideas to try

1 Type in the simple data-base with two fields and get it to work.

2 Consult your *User Manual* to help you to write LOAD and SAVE FILES routines.

3 Re-write the program so that you can choose any number of fields.

4 Develop the QUERY routine so that it will search for two words, only printing out the row if both words occur.

5 Use the sub-string search routine from *Monsters, Castles and Funny Machines* (see page 12) to give your QUERY routine more variety.

A competition scoreboard

In almost every sporting event you can think of, the scores, times and results can be displayed on a television screen using a computer.

Before you try to write a scoreboard program of your own you must think carefully about what you want it to do. Will it be for just one kind of event, like a running race? Will you want to use it for different events on different occasions? Will it record scores or times? Will each contestant have more than one score?

Here is a flow diagram for a computer scoreboard:

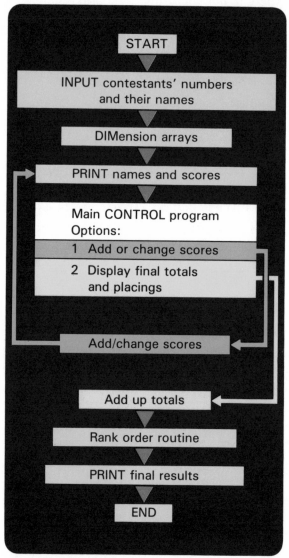

START

INPUT contestants' numbers and their names

DIMension arrays

PRINT names and scores

Main CONTROL program
Options:
1 Add or change scores
2 Display final totals and placings

Add/change scores

Add up totals

Rank order routine

PRINT final results

END

Notice that once the arrays have been DIMensioned the whole thing is organised by the main CONTROL program. This time only two options are offered, either to add or change scores, or to display the final totals and placings. Each time a new score is added, the whole scoreboard is updated and printed on the screen. When all scores are complete the final totals are calculated and then placed in rank-order with the highest score at the top and the lowest at the bottom. Finally the full results and placings are printed on the screen.

The example we are going to look at is for a competition involving two elements, giving each contestant two scores. It could be for gymnastics or athletics, but it could be used just as easily for a quiz. You will see as we go along how to adapt the ideas for your own use and how to alter the program to change the number of elements. Here is the first routine:

```
10 REM ***COMPETITION SCOREBOARD***
20 REM ***FOR TWO ELEMENTS***
30 CLS
40 REM --------------------------
50 REM**ENTER CONTESTANTS**
60 REM --------------------------
70 INPUT "HOW MANY CONTESTANTS ",N
80 DIM A$(N): DIM B(N,4)
90 REM ** B(N,1)= CONTESTANT NUMBER**
100 REM ** B(N,2)= SCORE NUMBER 1**
110 REM ** B(N,3)= SCORE NUMBER 2**
120 REM ** B(N,4)= TOTAL
130 FOR M=1 TO N
140 LET B(M,1)=M
150 PRINT "NAME OF CONTESTANT NUMBER ";M
160 INPUT A$(M)
170 NEXT M
180 CLS
```

```
HOW MANY CONTESTANTS ?4
NAME OF CONTESTANT NUMBER 1
?KATHERINE
NAME OF CONTESTANT NUMBER 2
?SARAH
NAME OF CONTESTANT NUMBER 3
?JANE
NAME OF CONTESTANT NUMBER 4
?SUSAN
```

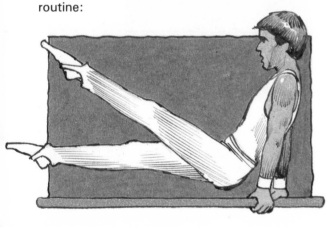

Notice this time that there are two arrays:

A$(N) is for the contestants' names and B(N,4) is for the scores and results.

Why do you think it is necessary to have a separate array for the scores?

If you want to change the number of competition elements then you will need to change B(N,4), but do not forget to include columns for the contestants' numbers and the final scores. The number of scores that you can display, and the amount of room for each score will depend upon the width of your screen display. This could be 20, 32, 40, 64 or 80 characters depending on which computer you are using.

How to space out your screen display

You will probably need to allow five spaces for each score, eg POINTS with two decimal places – 14.45, or TIMES in minutes and seconds – 2.59. Then you will need another two spaces before the next column. That makes seven spaces in all.

1 Decide how much room you need for the names and/or contestants' numbers, (say X).
2 Allow seven spaces for each score.
3 Your TAB positions will be: (X + 7),(X + 14),(X + 21),(X + 28) and so on.
4 You will soon see how many individual scores you can display across the screen at any one time.

But remember, when you print out the final totals and placings you will need two extra columns.

Look at this routine. It prints out the headings and scores for two elements together with the contestants' names and numbers. See if you can work out how many spaces are available for the names:

```
190 REM --------------------------
200REM**PRINT NAMES AND CURRENT SCORES**
210 REM --------------------------
220 PRINT"No. ";TAB(3);"NAME";TAB(15);"1";
225 PRINT TAB(21);"2"
230 PRINT"*********************************"
240 FOR P=1 TO N
250PRINT;B(P,1);TAB(3);A$(P);TAB(15);B(P,2);
255 PRINT TAB(21);B(P,3)
260 NEXT P
```

If your screen is only 20 or 32 characters wide you will need to leave out the contestants' names and just print the numbers.

Here is a suitable routine for the Spectrum:

```
220 PRINT "NO.";TAB 4;"1";TAB
11;"2";TAB 18;"TOTAL";TAB 25;"PLACE"
```

Now you should be able to write lines 230 to 260 for yourself.

The main control program

Look back at the flow-diagram. You will see that the CONTROL program is very simple. It offers just two choices. Try this as a starter:

```
280 REM --------------------------
290 REM OPTIONS ROUTINE
300 REM --------------------------
310 PRINT "PRESS 'S' TO ADD OR CHANGE SCORES"
320 PRINT "PRESS 'T' FOR FINAL TOTALS."
```

and then, using INPUT and IF-THEN, write lines 330 to 350 for yourself. It is best not to use INKEY$ or GET$ for this routine because they do not allow you to correct mistakes easily.

Sinclair users may need to use four lines for this routine because they do not have the IF-THEN-ELSE facility.

Adding and changing scores

Using the same routine to do two jobs saves time and space. Once a score has been entered, it is useful to be able to change it at any time. If a new score is typed in it will always replace the previous one. When you first run the program, all scores are automatically set to zero. We can change any of them as often as we like. Look at this routine:

```
360 REM -------------------------
370 REM ADD/CHANGE SCORES ROUTINE
380 REM -------------------------
390 PRINT "CONTESTANT NUMBER ";
400 INPUT Q
410 INPUT "ELEMENT ",E
420 INPUT "SCORE ",B(Q,E+1)
430 GOTO180
```

Why does the score go into column E + 1 ?

```
No. NAME          1    2
******************************************
1  KATHERINE    8.55  0
2  SARAH          0   0
3  JANE           0   0
4  SUSAN          0   0


PRESS 'S' TO ADD OR CHANGE SCORES
PRESS 'T' FOR FINAL TOTALS.
```

Entering the contestant number and the element number automatically tells the computer which row and which column to go to in the array. When the score has been entered, the program returns to line 180 (see page 25) to clear the screen before re-printing the names and updating the scores.

If you have typed the program in so far, you should be able to enter the names and scores, and have a full display of the current scores at all times. Do not continue until you are satisfied that this works. Here is a sample printout from a gymnastics competition. It has two elements and four contestants. The individual scores are complete, but the final totals and placings have not been worked out:

EACH TIME YOU ENTER 'S' YOU CAN ADD OR CHANGE A SCORE. WHEN ALL THE SCORES ARE ENTERED THE SCREEN DISPLAY WILL LOOK LIKE THE ONE AT THE TOP OF THE PAGE.

Adding up the totals

This routine is very simple. Starting with row 1 of the array, add the scores together and store them in row 4. This is then repeated for each row:

```
440 REM -------------------------
450 REM ** ADD UP TOTALS ROUTINE**
460 REM -------------------------
470 FOR M=1 TO N
480 B(M,4)=B(M,2)+B(M,3)
490 NEXT M
```

If you only have one element you do not need this routine at all. If you have more than two elements then you only need to change line 480. Remember that N is the number of rows in the array, one for each contestant.

Placing the scores in rank-order

The rank-order routine is quite complicated. It uses a "ripple-sort".

```
500 REM --------------------------
510 REM ** RANK ORDER ROUTINE **
520 REM --------------------------
530 FOR S=1 TO N-1
540 LET M=0
550 FOR I=1 TO N-S
560 IF B(I,4)>=B(I+1,4) THEN 680
570 REM ** S1=SCORE NO. 1 **
580 REM ** S2=SCORE NO. 2 **
590 REM ** X=TOTAL SCORE **
600 REM ** Y$=CONTESTANTS NAME **
610 REM ** Z=CONTESTANTS NUMBER **
620 X=B(I,4):Y$=A$(I):S1=B(I,2):S2=B(I,3):Z=B(I,1)
630 B(I,4)=B(I+1,4):A$(I)=A$(I+1):B(I,2)=B(I+1,2)
640 B(I,3)=B(I+1,3):B(I,1)=B(I+1,1)
650 B(I+1,4)=X:A$(I+1)=Y$:B(I+1,2)=S1
660 B(I+1,3)=S2:B(I+1,1)=Z
670 M=1
680 NEXT I
690 IF M=0 THEN 710
700 NEXT S
710 CLS
```

The routine sorts the total scores into descending order, the smallest scores sinking to the bottom. It starts by pointing an 'index' (I) at row 1.

It then advances, row by row, comparing the score in each row with the score in the row ahead of it. If the first score is lower than the second score it swops them over. After one complete 'sweep' it begins again stopping one row short because the lowest score has already sunk to the bottom. This continues until all scores are placed in rank-order. Look at line 560. This is where the total scores are compared. Notice that the first and second scores are not compared, nor are the names and contestant numbers. However, if two total scores are swopped, the whole row is swopped with them. This is all done by lines 620 to 660.

If you want more than two elements they will have to be labelled S1, S2, S3, S4....and so on. Do not attempt this until you understand how the 'ripple-sort' works.

The final printout

Your final printout will contain two extra columns, the total scores and the places. You will have to add two more TAB positions for these. Apart from that, the printout routine is the same as that used earlier. But this time, when you print out the contents of the two arrays, the results will appear in rank-order. Here is the routine:

```
720 REM ---------------------------
730 REM**PRINT OUT FINAL RESULTS**
740 REM ---------------------------
750 PRINT"No. ";TAB(3);"Name";TAB(15);"1";
755 PRINT TAB(21);"2";
760 PRINT TAB(27);"Total";TAB(34);"Place"
770 PRINT"***************************************"
780 FOR I=1 TO N
790 PRINT;B(I,1);TAB(3);A$(I);TAB(15);B(I,2);
795 PRINT TAB(21);B(I,3);
800 PRINT TAB(27);B(I,4);TAB(34);I
810 NEXT I
820 END
```

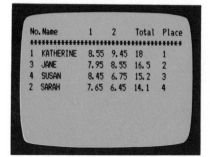

```
No. Name        1     2    Total  Place
****************************************
1   KATHERINE  8.55  9.45  18     1
3   JANE       7.95  8.55  16.5   2
4   SUSAN      8.45  6.75  15.2   3
2   SARAH      7.65  6.45  14.1   4
```

AND HERE IS THE RESULT!

Using a printer

It is always useful to have a printed copy of the results of your competition. This is particularly so in case of breakdown or power failure. It would be very awkward indeed if, during the competition, there was a power cut or somebody accidentally pulled out the plug. If you have a printer available, it can print each score as it is typed in. When the competition is over and the scores and places are calculated, it can provide as many copies of the results as are required. So remember, if you are going to use a program of this kind for a real competition:

1 Fully test the program in every way first.
2 Add extra lines to trap all possible operator errors.
3 Make some provision for a permanent record of all scores as they arise.

If you do not have a printer, then a pencil and paper will do.

Some ideas to try

1 Type in this program and get it to work.
2 Modify the program for a different number of elements.
3 Re-write the program so that it will accept a different number of elements each time it is used.
4 Try it out at a real competition with your friends, or at school.

End of term sports day